THE ANTARCTICA BOOK
LIVING IN THE FREEZER
by Dr Mark Norman

black dog

Dr Mark Norman is
a research scientist
at Museum Victoria.
He has travelled to Antarctica
numerous times, on one trip the
ship getting trapped
in sea ice for 47 days.

Photo credits

Mark Norman
pp. 2, 12, 13, 15, 28, 29

Norbert Wu
pp. 6, 8, 10, 20, 21, 24, 25,
back cover

Lyn Irvine (Images of Antarctica)
front cover

**Australian Government
Antarctic Division:**
Gerry Nash p. 27
Fiona Scott p. 24

Julian Finn p. 16

Greg Jordan p. 28

Glen Tepke p. 23

Getty Images
pp. i, ii, 2, 3, 16, 19

Guillaume Dargaud
pp. 1, 14, 17, 18, 19, 22, 30

Corbis pp. 7, 11

Kat Bolstad p. 9

**Ministry of Fisheries,
New Zealand** p. 9

Lukasz Michalczyk p. 26

Peter Boyer p. 5 (maps)

First published in 2007 by
black dog books
15 Gertrude Street
Fitzroy Vic 3065
Australia
61 + 3 + 9419 9406
61 + 3 + 9419 1214 (fax)
dog@bdb.com.au

Dr Mark Norman asserts the moral right to be identified as author of this Work.

Copyright text © Dr Mark Norman 2007

All rights reserved. Apart from any fair dealing for the purposes of study, research, criticism or review, as permitted under the Copyright Act, no part of this book may be reproduced by any process, stored in a retrieval system, or transmitted in any form, without permission of the copyright owner. All inquiries should be made to the publisher at the address above.

black dog books would like to thank Professor Patrick Quilty for his thorough factual check of this book.

Designed by Blue Boat Design
Printed and bound in China by Everbest

National Library of Australia
cataloguing-in-publication data:
Norman, Mark

    The Antarctica book — living in the freezer.

    Includes index.
    For primary school students.
    ISBN 9781921167867.

    1. Animals – Antarctica - Juvenile literature. I. Title.

    591.9989

10 9 8 7 6 5 4 3   7 8 9/0

CONTENTS

ANTARCTICA IS A WEIRD PLACE	2
WHAT'S IT LIKE IN ANTARCTICA?	4
THE WORLD'S BIGGEST ANIMALS	
Blue Whale	6
Humpback Whale	7
DEEP-SEA GLADIATORS	
Sperm Whale	8
Colossal Squid	9
THE SMALLER WHALES	
Minke Whale	10
Orcas	11
THE BIG SEALS	
Southern Elephant Seal	12
Leopard Seal	13
SMALLER SEALS	
Weddell Seal	14
Crabeater Seal	15
BIG BIRDS	
Wandering Albatross	16
Southern Giant Petrel	17
ANTARCTIC PENGUINS	
Emperor Penguin	18
Adelie Penguin	19
UNDER THE WATER	
Antarctic Icefish	20
Antarctic Sea Spider	21
THE LITTLEST BIRDS	
Snow Petrel	22
Wilsons Storm Petrel	23
LITTLE SHRIMP AND TINY PLANTS	
Ice Algae	24
Antarctic Krill	25
THE TINIEST ANTARCTIC CRITTERS	
Tardigrades or Water Bears	26
Antarctic Mite	27
ANTARCTICA: PAST, PRESENT AND FUTURE	28
GLOSSARY	30
INDEX	30

ANTARCTICA IS A WEIRD PLACE

At the bottom of our planet is a very strange land known as Antarctica. It is the coldest place on earth. It's surrounded by sea so you can't drive there — you have to go by ship or plane. There are no cities — the only people staying there all year are a few scientists living in research stations.

It is very, very cold — the lowest temperature ever recorded there is -89°C, which is 70°C colder than in your freezer! If human skin is exposed to this sort of temperature, the skin quickly dies and goes black from frostbite. Many early explorers lost fingers and toes to frostbite. When it's this cold, the water vapour in your breath freezes instantly and falls to the ground as flakes of ice.

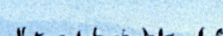

So how do animals and plants survive in this freezing place? All sorts of creatures live in Antarctica, and each has adapted to the extreme conditions in its own special way. There are no forests or grass plains in Antarctica — almost everything is ice. There is not a single tree in 13 million square kilometres! Tiny mosses and algae are the only land plants, surviving by sheltering in crevices and under rocks.

Most of Antarctica's animal life lives in the sea or on the very edges of the icy land. Antarctic waters are so rich with food that huge whales can feast there for months and live off the fat for the rest of the year.

Many amazing creatures are found in Antarctica, from the world's tiniest and toughest animals to the largest animal that has ever lived on earth.

WHAT'S IT LIKE IN ANTARCTICA?

Antarctica is a huge land. Over millions of years of cold temperatures, so much snow has fallen that it has formed a massive ice sheet over most of this land. In some places it is almost 5km thick! Antarctica's ice is always moving. Near the coast it forms slow-moving rivers of ice called glaciers. They run into the sea where they break up into floating icebergs. Some Antarctic icebergs are up to 100km long. Most of them slowly melt, break apart and drift out to sea.

Just like other countries, Antarctica has varying terrain. It has tall mountain ranges, active volcanoes, big bays and many small offshore islands.

Despite all the snow, it is actually very dry in Antarctica — there is less rain than in the Sahara desert! In some places the winds make it so dry that not even snow can fall. These places are known as 'dry valleys'. Scientists have found mummified seals in some of these valleys. The seals crawled in 5000 years ago, died and dried up, never rotting away.

In the dark Antarctic winter, it gets so cold that the surface of the sea freezes solid. This is known as 'pack ice' or 'sea ice'. The frozen sea in winter covers an area bigger than Antarctica itself. In spring, the ice starts melting and by February most of the sea has melted. In some bays, the sea stays frozen solid through summer, connected to the land. This is known as 'fast ice'.

Antarctica is a very different place to the area known as the Arctic. Antarctica is a frozen land surrounded by sea, home to penguins, seals, albatrosses and whales. The Arctic is a frozen sea surrounded by land, home to polar bears, puffins, reindeer, Arctic foxes and Arctic owls. These two very different groups of animals are at opposite ends of the world and never meet except in zoos or cartoons. The word 'Antarctica' actually means 'the opposite of the Arctic'.

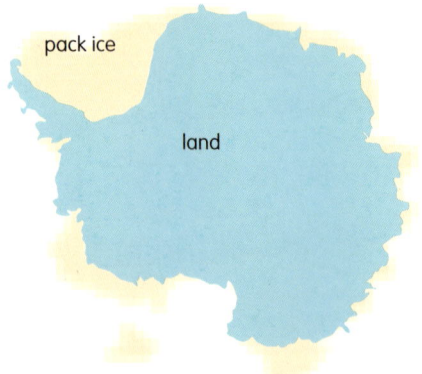

Antarctica in Summer

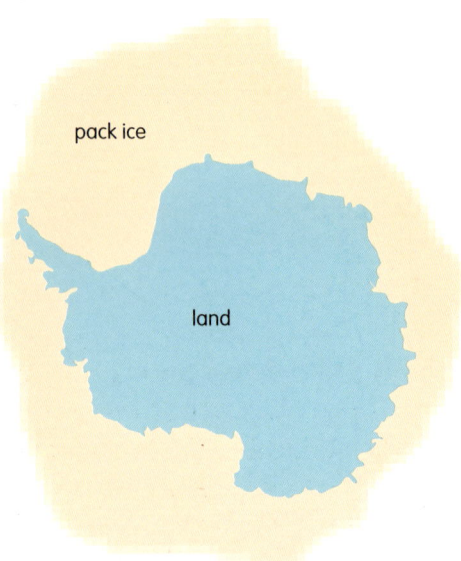

Antarctica in Winter

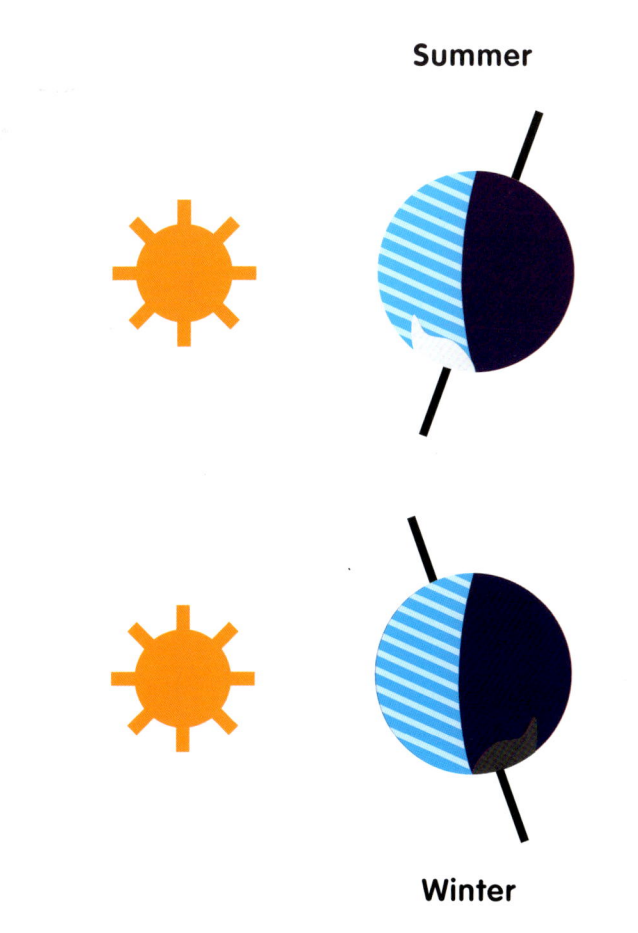

Summer

Winter

Antarctica is at the bottom end of the earth. The earth spins at an angle to the sun, this affects the daylight in Antarctica. In summer all of Antarctica is aimed towards the sun, so it is never dark. In the middle of winter, Antarctica is facing away from the sun and is in 24 hour darkness. In spring and autumn there is day and night like normal.

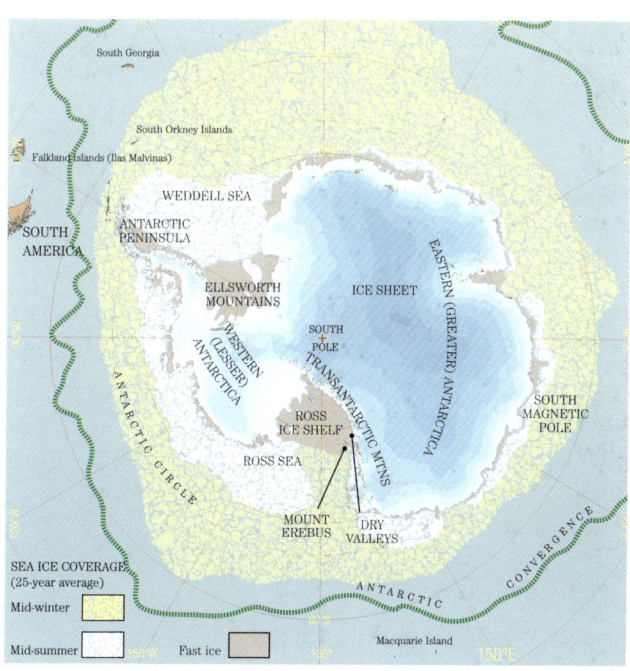

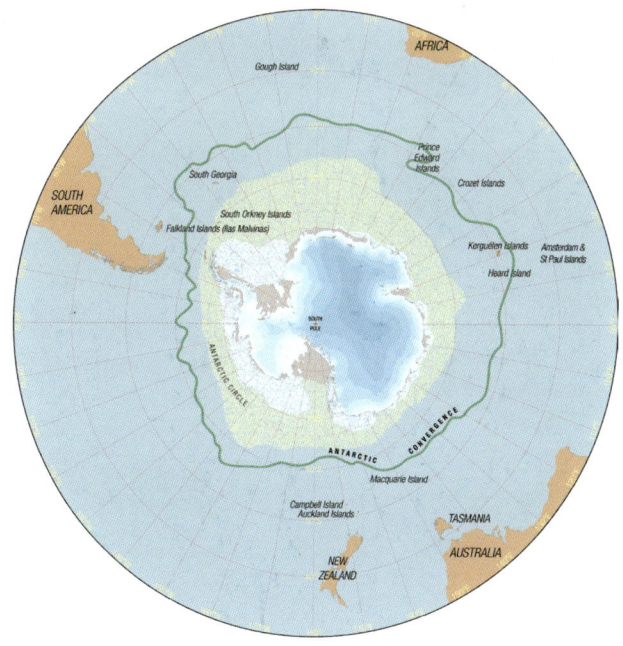

THE WORLD'S BIGGEST ANIMALS
BLUE WHALE
(Balaenoptera musculus)

Blue Whales are the biggest animals that have ever lived on earth — even bigger than the biggest dinosaur.

Every summer Blue Whales travel to Antarctica to feast on huge amounts of small shrimp known as krill. One Blue Whale can eat 6 tonnes of krill a day.

When the whales have eaten enough krill to get really fat, they head for warmer water to breed. They don't stay in Antarctica to have their babies because the water is too cold for the calves to survive.

Humans used to hunt Blue Whales using ships and harpoons. Scientists think there were once about 250,000 Blue Whales in the world before big-scale whaling started. Today, they think there are around 6000 left. These whales are now fully protected, so no one can hunt them anymore.

Predators:	Young can be attacked by Orcas.
Feeding:	Krill, some other small crustaceans, and squid.
Migration:	Antarctica in summer, into warmer waters in winter. Breeding areas unknown, probably tropical waters.

30m, 150 tonnes

Humpback and Blue Whales belong to a group of whales known as 'baleen whales'. Instead of teeth, they have baleen plates — sheets of modified hair that look like flat boards. These whales feed by sucking in sea water, up to 50 tonnes in one gulp, which is full of krill. They squirt the water out through the baleen plates like a sieve and trap all the wriggling krill inside the mouth — just like straining pasta.

HUMPBACK WHALE
(Megaptera novaeangliae)

When whales breathe they blow a big jet of water into the air, known as a 'spout'. The shape of the water spout differs for each whale. Some go straight up in a single spout, some go to one side, Southern Right Whales have two spouts.

The Humpback Whale gets its name for the hump on its back with a very small fin. It has extremely long side flippers with bumps along the front edge. Each flipper is 5m long. This whale seems to like performing — rolling, leaping out of the water and waving its flippers. Humpbacks have a special way of getting the fish or krill together in one group. It is called 'bubble netting'. The whale dives below the krill and swims in circles, blowing through its blowhole. As its breath rises it forms a circle of tiny bubbles and all the krill move into the middle. The whale then opens its mouth and swims straight up the middle to eat all the krill in one go.

Predators: Orcas, large sharks.

Feeding: Schooling small fish, krill, other small crustaceans.

Migration: Summers in Antarctica, winter to tropical waters to breed.

18m, 40 tonnes

DEEP-SEA GLADIATORS
SPERM WHALE
(Physeter macrocephalus)

Sperm Whales have a large square head with one big nostril on the tip and a funny skinny lower jaw.

Large male Sperm Whales travel south to Antarctica every summer to dive for Colossal Squid and other big squid. They are kept warm by a layer of blubber up to 30cm thick. Female and young Sperm Whales stay further north where it's warmer. Sperm Whales are excellent divers — they can dive to a depth of 2km and stay underwater for up to two hours, all on a single breath! They find their food in the dark water by making clicking sounds and listening for the sound waves bouncing back, just like radar. When they locate their food they grab it with their long, thin bottom jaw, which is full of large teeth. They don't have any upper teeth. Sperm Whales can eat huge amounts. One was found with 18,000 small squid in its stomach.

The long scars around the mouth of Sperm Whales can be caused by the sharp hooks of the Colossal Squid.

Sperm Whales belong to a group of whales known as the 'toothed whales'. They have obvious teeth for grabbing squid and fish. Sperm Whales only have teeth in their lower jaw. Some other toothed whales have only four or even two teeth.

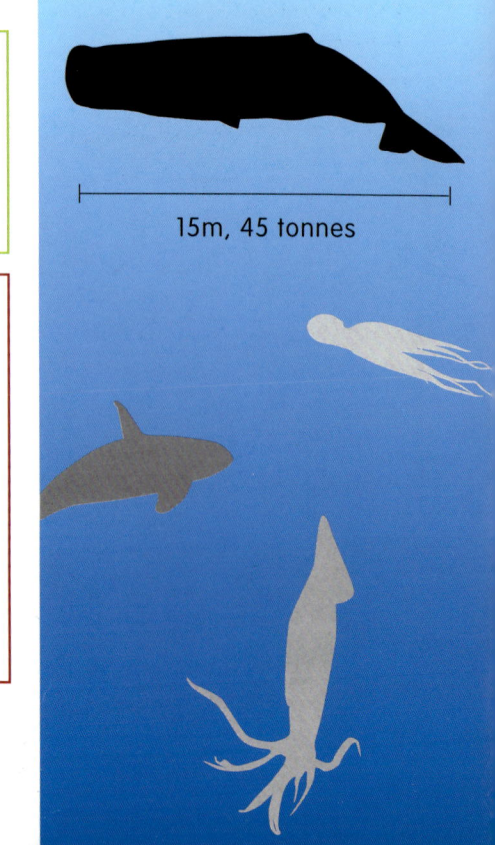

Predators: Orcas.

Feeding: Colossal, Giant and small squids, deep sea fish and octopuses.

Migration: Only the big males come to Antarctica in summer. In winter they go back to tropical waters to meet up with the females.

15m, 45 tonnes

COLOSSAL SQUID
(Mesonychoteuthis hamiltoni)

Animals without a backbone are known as 'invertebrates'. The biggest invertebrate animal in the world is a squid and it lives in the cold waters of Antarctica. The Colossal Squid live in waters so cold and deep, that very little is known about them. Young Colossal Squid have been caught in nets at 2km deep. Young have also been found in the stomachs of Sperm Whales. Only one adult Colossal Squid has ever been found by scientists, captured by fishermen in 2007.

The Colossal Squid is huge. Its body is the size of a small car and it has eight big arms and two longer tentacles. If you made calamari rings out of a Colossal Squid, the rings would be as big as truck tyres. It has the biggest eyes in the world — as big as basketballs!

Other squids and octopuses live in Antarctic seas including the large jelly-like octopus known as Megaleledone (*Megaleledone setebos*) (3m arm span) and the see-through Antarctic Glass Squid (*Galiteuthis glacialis*) (60cm long).

Predators: Sperm Whales.
Feeding: Squid and fish.
Migration: Young are found in slightly warmer waters. The largest animals have only been found in Antarctica.

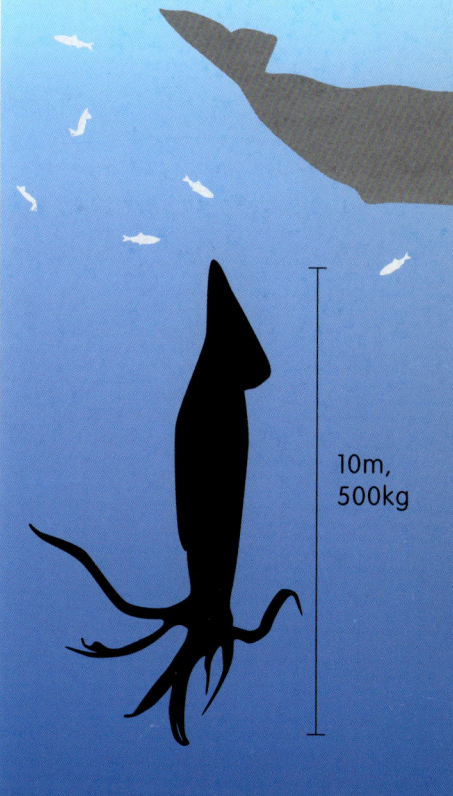

10m, 500kg

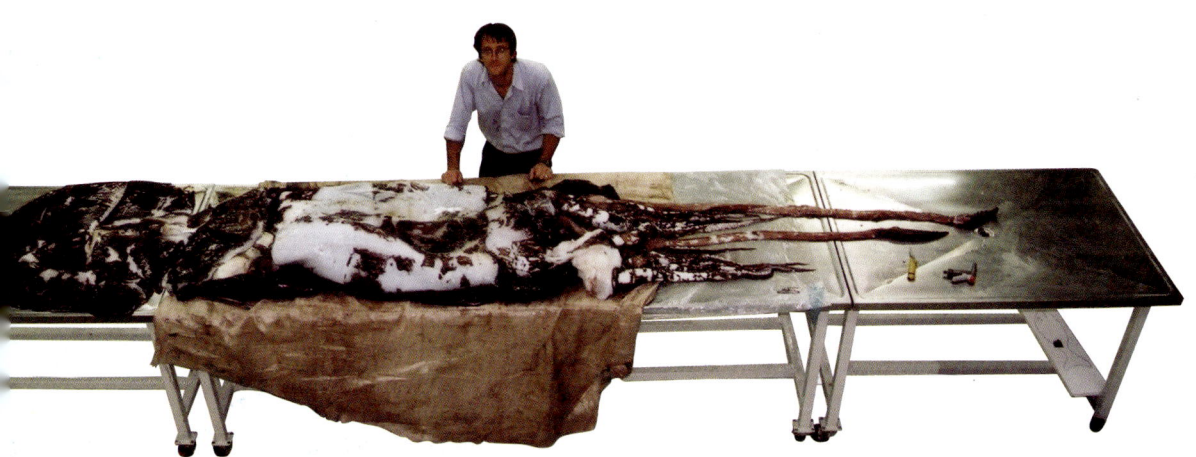

THE SMALLER WHALES
MINKE WHALES
(Balaenoptera acutorostrata)

Minke Whales are the smallest of the 'baleen whales'. Just like the Blue Whale, they have baleen plates instead of teeth.

Minke Whales are very loud — loud enough to give you a headache if you were too close. They grunt and rumble to communicate with other whales a great distance away.

Minke Whales are the most common whales on earth. Scientists estimate there could be up to one million in the Antarctic alone. Every year they come to Antarctica to feast on krill, then cruise north to spend their winter holidays lounging around in warmer waters.

Most countries in the world have agreed to stop whale hunting. But some countries are still hunting Minke Whales in the Antarctic.

Predators: Orcas, sharks.
Feeding: Krill, small fish.
Migration: Summers in Antarctica, winters in temperate and tropical waters.

10m, 10 tonnes

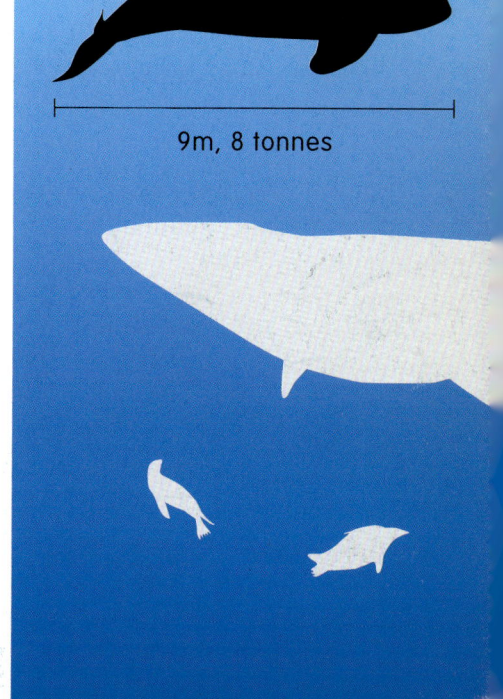

Predators:	No known predators.
Feeding:	Whales, dolphins, seals, penguins, seabirds, fish, squid.
Migration:	Antarctica in summer, places like South Africa, New Zealand and southern Australia in winter.

9m, 8 tonnes

Orcas are also known as Killer Whales and are like the lions of Antarctica. They hunt in packs, known as pods. They need to be very clever to catch penguins and seals that hide above the water on the frozen sea ice. Some Orcas jump in the air and splash water over floating pack ice to wash the seals into the sea. They can even jump onto the frozen sea ice and break off the edge to knock penguins into the water or smash up through thinner ice and grab them from below.

Orcas, like Sperm Whales, are toothed whales. They can live up to 100 years, migrating every summer from the warm waters of the Pacific and Atlantic oceans to Antarctica. They are easy to identify on their travels as the male Orca has a very tall fin that can be seen from a distance.

Other small Antarctic whales are the Arnoux's Beaked Whale (10m long) and the Southern Bottle-nosed Whale (7.5m long). Both of these have long, round snouts and four small teeth sticking out the front of their mouths. The tiny Hourglass Dolphin (1.6m long) is the only dolphin that swims in Antarctic seas. Its name comes from the pattern on its body which looks like an old-fashioned hourglass with sand inside.

ORCAS
(Orcinus orca)

Elephant seals are the biggest seals in the world. They are excellent divers. They can dive 2km into the deep sea where it is so dark you could not see your hand in front of your face. With their super-sensitive eyes they can see the weak light given off by glowing deep-sea squids.

On land, Elephant Seals are very awkward. They are so fat that they shuffle everywhere, looking like a sock full of custard going for a walk.

Elephant Seals have only a few peg-like teeth, all they need to grab soft squid. The big male seals can inflate their noses to make loud trumpet calls. They use these when they're fighting other males. They bump into each other with their flabby fat chests and try to bite each other through their thick skin.

Predators: Orcas, Leopard Seals.

Feeding: Squid, fish.

Migration: Live on Antarctic and subantarctic islands year round, feed closer to Antarctica in summer. Young males can get to South Africa, Australia and New Zealand in winter.

5m, 4 tonnes

THE BIG SEALS
SOUTHERN ELEPHANT SEAL
(Mirounga leonina)

LEOPARD SEAL
(Hydrurga leptonyx)

The Leopard Seal gets its name from its spotted coat. But these seals are more like the crocodiles of Antarctica. They have long jaws and lots of long sharp teeth. They hunt other seals and penguins by sneaking around ice floes or in front of penguin colonies with only their eyes and the tips of their nostrils showing above the water surface. Leopard Seals can also smash up through the ice to grab Adelie Penguins and Crabeater Seal pups.

Blubber and fur keep Antarctic seals warm. Every year Elephant Seals come ashore to moult. This is where they shed all their old fur and grow new fur. They can't swim until the new fur is ready, so they lie around sleeping all day. They get itchy as the new fur grows, so they like to roll around in mud and poo to stop the itchiness.

Predators: Orcas.

Feeding: Seal pups, penguins, seabirds, squid, fish, krill.

Migration: Summer amongst the pack ice, winter around subantarctic islands.

3m, 350kg

SMALLER SEALS
WEDDELL SEAL
(Leptonychotes weddelli)

The colour pattern of these seals can act as camouflage when they lie on rocky beaches in summer, hiding from Leopard Seals or Orcas.

Weddell Seals are one of the toughest seals in the world. They spend the whole year in Antarctic waters, even when the surface of the sea freezes solid. They use their strong buckteeth to scrape open a breathing hole through the ice so they can keep diving for food and still breathe.

Weddell Seals are great swimmers, diving down 750m deep to catch fish and octopus. Scientists have timed their dives and found they can hold their breath for 73 minutes! Humans are lucky to make 2 minutes! The same scientists attached radiotrackers to the seals and found they can swim up to 12km under the ice away from their air hole and back again.

In the middle of winter the air temperature can be -30°C, but these seals keep warm by staying in the water, which is still a very chilly -1.8°C.

Predators: Orcas, Leopard Seals.

Feeding: Large fish (to 1.5m), squid, octopus and larger shrimp.

Migration: Remain amongst the pack ice year round.

3m, 500kg

CRABEATER SEAL
(Lobodon carcinophagus)

Other seals in Antarctica are Ross Seals that live and dive among the sea ice and Antarctic Fur Seals (1.6m, 130kg) that inhabit rocky islands around Antarctica. In the 1800s, millions of these seals were killed for their fur. Their numbers are now beginning to increase.

Scientists think Crabeater Seals are one of the most common big mammals on earth — second only to humans. They estimate that there are up to 15 million of these seals in Antarctica.

Crabeater Seals don't eat crabs! They got their name from early explorers who found the remains of red krill shrimp in the seals' stomachs and assumed they were chewed-up red crabs. These seals have special branching teeth that form a sieve when their mouth is closed. They use these to trap small krill in their mouths.

Female Crabeater Seals haul themselves up onto frozen sea ice to have their pups. For one month, the mother doesn't eat at all as she feeds the pup with thick oily milk. The pup quickly swells from 20kg to 110kg in just four weeks! Imagine getting five times bigger in just one month.

Predators: Orcas, Leopard Seals.

Feeding: Krill.

Migration: Remain amongst the pack ice year round.

2m, 220kg

BIG BIRDS
WANDERING ALBATROSS
(Diomedea exulans)

Wandering Albatrosses have the biggest wingspan of any bird in the world — up to 3.5m! Albatrosses are expert gliders, using the wind gusts coming up off waves to fly without flapping. When there's no wind they have to sit in the water and wait. Albatrosses even fly while sleeping by shutting down half their brain at a time.

When Wandering Albatrosses are young they can spend up to 3 years flying around the world and feeding at sea without ever touching land. They land on the sea surface to grab squid and fish and swim awkwardly underwater down to about 1m. They feed mainly at night to avoid being seen by sharks or toothed whales.

These albatrosses travel huge distances. In the 1800s, one caught off the coast of Chile in South America had a note tied around its neck saying it had been released 12 days earlier from a whaling ship 6000km away.

The Wandering Albatross takes several years to choose a mate but once it does, it stays with its partner for life, which can be up to 80 years.

3.5m wingspan, 11kg

Predators: Chicks taken by Giant Petrels and skuas. Adults taken by sharks outside Antarctica.

Feeding: Squid, some fish.

Migration: Fly right around the southern end of the world. Can fly more than 15,000km between breeding seasons.

Giant petrels are like the vultures of Antarctica. You have to be careful having a nap in the open in Antarctica. If you lie still for too long, Giant Petrels may come along and try to tear some flesh off you.

Their big heavy beaks are so sharp that they can cut through the thick skin of dead Elephant Seals and poke their heads in to eat the guts. They mainly eat dead or dying animals but will also steal eggs and kill seal pups and penguin chicks. Most Southern Giant Petrels are dark brown but about one in ten is pure white, which is good camouflage against the snow.

Have you ever wondered what birds drink when they spend so long in the sea? Seabirds drink seawater and then ooze salty snot out their nostrils to get rid of the extra salt. If we drank seawater we'd still die of thirst because of all the salt.

SOUTHERN GIANT PETREL
(Macronectes giganteus)

2m wingspan, 3kg

Predators: Leopard Seals. Sharks outside Antarctica.

Feeding: Scavengers. Dead seals, whales, penguins. Live penguin chicks and eggs.

Migration: Summers in Antarctica. As far north as Peru, South Africa, Australia and New Zealand in winter.

Emperor penguins are the biggest living penguin. At the beginning of winter, Emperor penguins walk a long way inland on the frozen sea. A mother Emperor penguin lays an egg, then she leaves in search of food. The father puts the egg on his feet and spends the entire dark cold winter standing on the ice. This isn't a trick — he's keeping the egg warm. To keep themselves warm, all the fathers huddle together through winter. They keep shuffling along, taking turns at being on the outside of the group where it is coldest.

As spring comes, the sea ice melts and breaks up and the chicks begin to hatch. The mother has travelled thousands of kilometres but she returns and finds her mate among the thousands of other penguins by hearing his particular call. The mother's belly will be full with food. The chick puts its head inside the mother's mouth and the mother vomits food directly into the chick's mouth. It sounds revolting to us but they love it. It's just like hot seafood soup.

ANTARCTIC PENGUINS
EMPEROR PENGUIN
(Aptenodytes forsteri)

Predators: Leopard Seals, Orcas.

Feeding: Fish, krill and squid.

Migration: Close to the Antarctic coast in summer. Females feed around outer pack ice in winter. Males stay locked in the ice near the Antarctic land through winter.

1m, 38kg

ADELIE PENGUIN
(Pygoscelis adeliae)

Adelie Penguins are cute and curious. They have black faces and a white ring around each black eye. Their beaks are covered in feathers to help keep them warm. Every spring in Antarctica they walk and slide hundreds of kilometres across the frozen sea ice to get to their breeding colonies. There they collect small stones to make their little nests.

Competition for stones is so fierce that the penguins resort to stone stealing and fights break out everywhere.

Adelie Penguins eat krill, which turns their poo red. Colonies of these penguins can be seen from the air because of the red poo.

Have you ever tried to stand or walk on ice? It is very slippery. Some penguins, like the Adelie and the Gentoo Penguin below, have a brushy tail that helps them balance on the ice and stops them from sliding backwards.

Predators:	Leopard Seals and Giant Petrels. Chicks taken by skuas.
Feeding:	Mainly krill with some squid and fish. Shallow divers.
Migration:	Close to Antarctic coast in summer. At outer edge of pack ice in winter.

70cm, 6kg

UNDER THE WATER
ANTARCTIC ICEFISH
(Channichthys rhinoceratus)

Not only do icefish look weird, they also have very unusual blood. It's clear and full of special anti-freeze chemicals.

If you put water in your freezer it turns to ice at 0°C. In the sea, because of all the salt, the water doesn't freeze solid until it gets down to -1.8°C. This means that animals swimming in this water need special ways to prevent their blood freezing. Seals and penguins have warm blood, lots of blubber and fur or feathers to stop them freezing. The anti-freeze in the blood of Antarctic icefish helps, but they still must be very careful. If they come into contact with ice it makes them that little bit colder and they become snap frozen. People catching icefish through holes in the ice say they freeze solid the instant they come out of the water into the colder air.

Icefish typically live on the sea floor, leaping up to grab passing fish and shrimp.

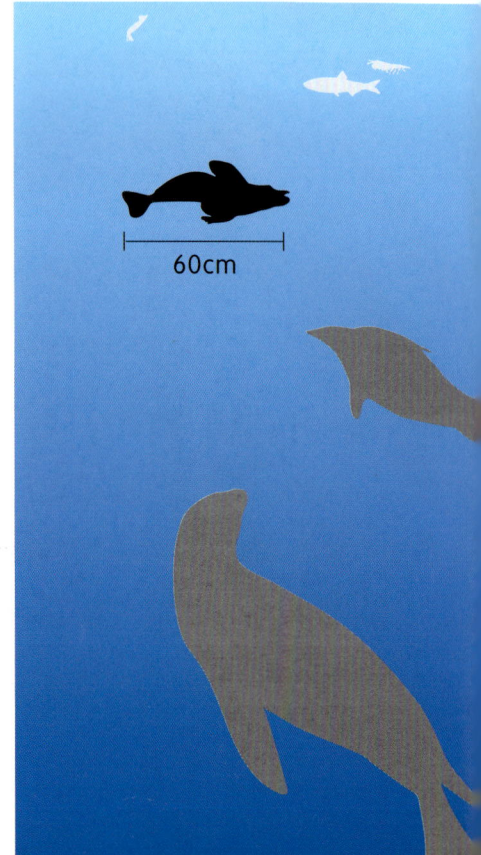

Predators: Antarctic Fur Seals, Gentoo Penguins.

Feeding: Fish, krill and large shrimp.

Migration: Unknown.

60cm

Sea spiders look like giant daddy-long-leg spiders. They are not related to land spiders but are in their own special group known as 'pycnogonids'. Some species have eight legs while others have ten or twelve. Their central body is so tiny that their guts are squeezed inside their hollow legs. Their mouth is like a tube with little scissors at the tip. They bite their way through the sides of sea anemones and suck out the liquid. Male sea spiders carry their eggs around under their body like little bunches of grapes.

Sea spiders look scary, but their legs are not very strong. If they came out of the water, they would struggle to stand up.

Many of the animals that live underwater in Antarctica live for a very long time. One starfish lived for 39 years and one limpet lived for 100 years! Because the water is so cold, the animals move very slowly and take a long time to grow.

ANTARCTIC SEA SPIDER
(Colossendeis megalonyx)

Predators: Unknown.
Feeding: Sea anemones and soft corals.
Migration: Occurs on the sea floor from 3m to 5km deep.

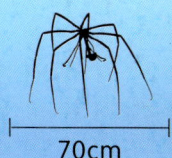

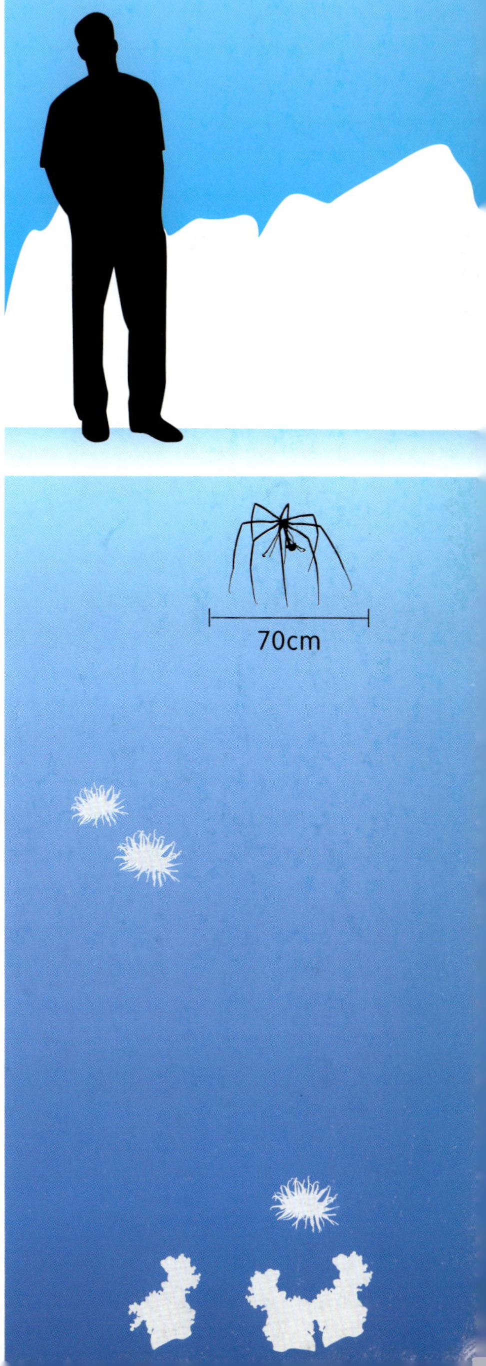

70cm

THE LITTLEST BIRDS
SNOW PETREL
(Pagodroma nivea)

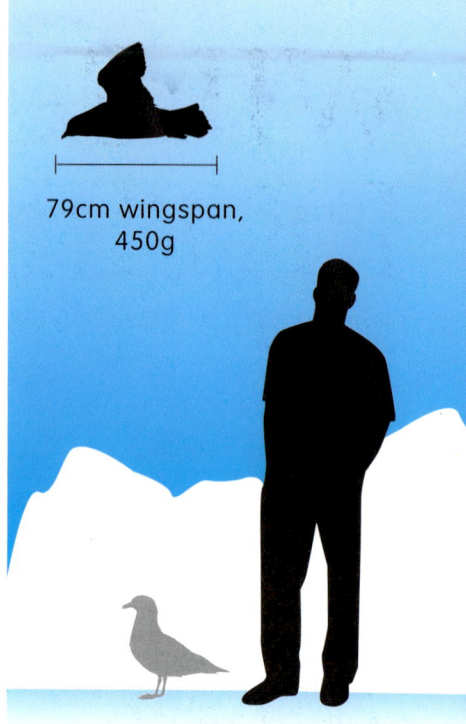

79cm wingspan, 450g

Predators:	Chicks taken by skuas.
Feeding:	Mainly squid, fish and krill.
Migration:	Remain near the edge of the pack ice year round.

Snow Petrels are pure white. When they fly against snowy backgrounds or past icebergs, all you can see is two small black eyes and a black beak flying past. Of all the birds in the world, Snow Petrels nest the closest to the South Pole. They hide from deadly skuas and Giant Petrels by flying up to 185km inland to find small caves in the tips of submerged mountains sticking up through the thick ice sheet. Snow Petrels feed among the pack ice and near icebergs where waves slapping against the ice can bring small fish and shrimp near the surface.

WILSONS STORM PETREL

(Oceanites oceanicus)

42cm wingspan, 50g

Wilsons Storm Petrels are like the tiny fluttering butterflies of the Antarctic. They may look weak but they're incredibly tough. Sailors tell of being in the middle of storms in huge rough seas and looking out the porthole to see these small birds fluttering effortlessly among the crashing waves, picking up food scraps from the water surface. Sometimes they pad their legs along the water while they flutter, making it look like they are walking on water. These birds fly huge distances each year. Some adults fly from North America to Antarctica every summer, flying back every winter, a trip of more than 20,000 km!

Other Antarctic birds include the Antarctic Petrel and diving petrels. Skuas and Sheathbills are the scavengers of Antarctica, hunting chicks, eggs and sick or injured birds. The Sheathbill is named for its weird beak which has wide sides; perfect for stealing penguin eggs. The Sheathbill can run off without breaking the egg, as if in an egg and spoon race.

Predators:	Skuas, Giant Petrels, Kelp Gulls, sharks.
Feeding:	Krill, shrimp and fish, some squid.
Migration:	Migrate to north of the equator every winter.

There are no trees in Antarctica. No fruit, no vegetables, no meadows of grass, no forests. It's mostly ice. Nearly all the food in Antarctica comes from the sea. And the food for most Antarctic animals comes from the two tiny creatures shown here — a simple seaweed (ice algae) and a small shrimp (krill). It's amazing that two of the smallest creatures in the world make up the food for the largest animal that has ever lived on our planet — the Blue Whale.

LITTLE SHRIMP AND TINY PLANTS
ICE ALGAE
(Nitzschia stellata)

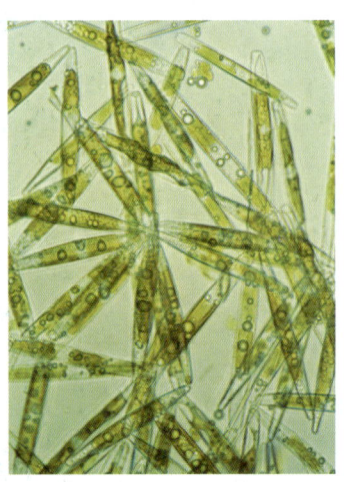

Ice algae are tiny plants that grow in big mats attached to the underside of the frozen sea ice. As the sun returns after the long dark months of winter, the light goes through the pack ice and lets the ice algae plants grow in pockets inside the ice. By the time the ice melts, these plants have formed a thick green layer in the ice.

These plants may be tiny, but they are very important to life in Antartica. They are food for the krill that swim upside down on the underside of the ice feeding on them. Because so much of the ocean freezes around Antarctica every winter, the ice makes a perfect place for these plants to thrive.

Predators: Krill.

Feeding: Grow using sunlight (photosynthesis).

Migration: Remain within and below frozen sea ice.

0.05mm

Krill are small, pink shrimp that feed on the ice algae that grows in frozen sea ice. Krill have special sharp legs called ice-rakers, which they use to scrape away the ice to get at the ice algae. In spring as the ice starts melting, the numbers of krill explode to form gigantic pink swarms of swimming shrimp. The sea turns pink and looks like a huge pink oil spill. Some krill swarms can be 60km long. Whales, dolphins, seals, penguins, albatrosses and other seabirds all love gorging on krill.

In winter, when there is no sun and no ice algae, krill eggs sink to the deep-sea floor at 2–3km deep. As they hatch, they slowly rise to the surface and live off their body reserves until the sun and algae return.

ANTARCTIC KRILL
(Euphausia superba)

Predators:	Whales, Crabeater Seals, penguins, sea birds and squids.
Feeding:	Ice algae.
Migration:	Shallow waters in summer, young hatch in deep waters in winter.

55mm

THE TINIEST ANTARCTIC CRITTERS

TARDIGRADES
OR WATER BEARS
(Acutuncus antarcticus)

Predators:	None known.
Feeding:	Algae and moss.
Migration:	Stay and freeze solid over winter.

Water bears are tiny animals that look like small barrels with legs. They live among Antarctic mosses in ice crevices. They are incredibly tough and can survive very low temperatures by squirting out all the moisture in their bodies and drying up. Their legs even suck in. When the weather gets warmer and they thaw out, they draw water back into their bodies, pop out their legs, wake up, walk off and start feeding again. They may live as long as 60–70 years. In controlled experiments, some have even recovered after being dipped in liquid helium (at -272°C!).

Many other tiny Antarctic creatures live among moss on land or in freshwater lakes. They include small shrimp-like animals called springtails, tiny worms called nematodes and microscopic single-cell animals called rotifers.

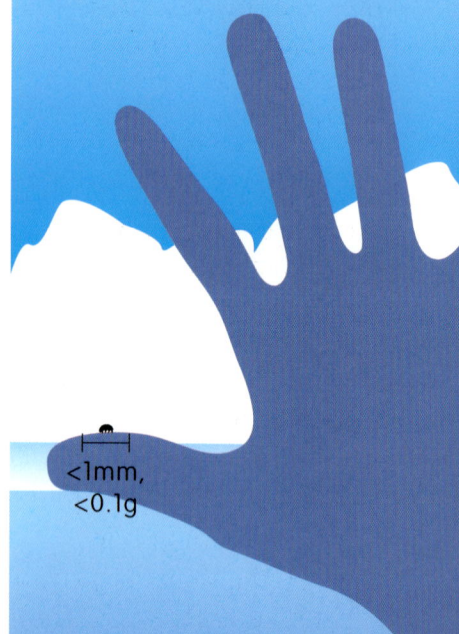

<1mm, <0.1g

Mites are tiny relatives of land spiders and lots of them live in Antarctica. This one lives in crevices among small plants called moss. Some feed on the plants, some feed on other mites. Like Tardigrades, they can be frozen solid through the winter and come back to life when it gets warmer.

One group of mites, known as nasal mites, has found the best spot to live. They crawl up the seal's nose and live in nice warm snot! They can look out at the view knowing they'll have warm air blowing over them. It's lucky that seals, such as Elephant Seals, close their nostrils when they dive down into the deep sea. Nasal mites probably move to new noses when the seals huddle together on beaches to stay warm.

ANTARCTIC MITE
(Nanorchestes antarcticus)

Predators:	None known.
Feeding:	Algae and moss.
Migration:	Stay and freeze solid over winter.

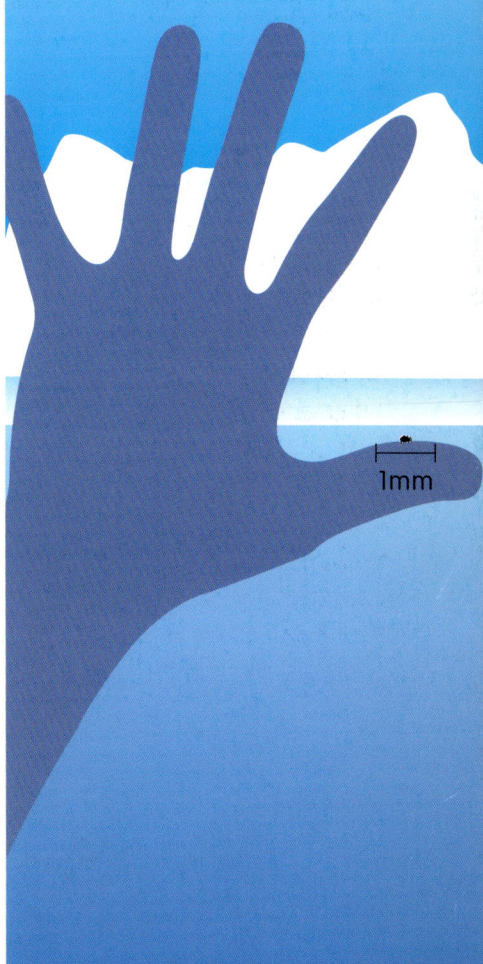

1mm

ANTARCTICA: PAST, PRESENT AND FUTURE

Antarctica in the past

Antarctica has not always been a frozen icy place. Millions of years ago the land part of Antarctica was joined with Africa, Australia and South America. This one big land, called Gondwana, was covered in forests and was home to dinosaurs, tree ferns, insects and primitive mammals. As Gondwana broke up, and ocean formed right round Antarctica, trapping the cold air and cooling the land until it froze. Today you can find fossils in Antarctica of the leaves of trees like Antarctic Myrtle Beech, a tree that still grows in Australia.

Antarctica today

Humans only discovered Antarctica 200 years ago. In the early days most came to hunt seals and whales; some came to explore. Today scientists in Antarctica carry out important research into the earth's climate. As ice freezes it traps air bubbles. Sample drilling through the ice sheet can bring up ice thousands of years old and show us how the weather is changing. Today people also come to Antarctica as tourists. They have to be carefully managed to make sure they don't disturb or harm the wildlife.

GLOSSARY AND INDEX

Glossary

anti-freeze: Special liquid put in car radiators to prevent them freezing solid in low temperatures.

body reserves: Fat stored in the body for when there is no food.

blubber: Thick layers of fat under the skin.

dry valleys: Places where it is so dry that it doesn't even snow, so the rocks are bare.

fast ice: Frozen sea ice that doesn't melt over summer.

glaciers: Rivers of compressed ice slowly flowing over mountains to the sea.

harpoons: The big spear used by whale hunters to kill whales.

ice sheet: The thick layer of ice that covers most of Antarctica.

icebergs: Huge pieces of ice that break off glaciers and float.

ice floes: Big flat pieces of frozen sea ice.

pack ice: Frozen sea ice, thickest and widest in winter.

protected: Animals that are not allowed to be fished or hunted.

scavengers: Animals that live off dead animals and scraps of food.

thaw out: To unfreeze when it gets warmer.

vultures: Large African birds that eat the bodies of dead animals.

wingspan: The distance from wing tip to wing tip when spread out.

Index

Adelie Penguin 19
albatross 16
algae 24
Antarctic Icefish 20
Antarctic Krill 25
Antarctic Mite 27
Antarctic Sea Spider 21
baleen whales 4, 5, 7, 8, 10
Blue Whale 6, 7, 10, 24
bubble netting 7
Colossal Squid 8, 9
Crabeater Seal 15, 25
Emperor Penguin 18
Humpback Whale 7
Ice Algae 24
ice sheet 4, 22, 28, 29
icefish 20
Killer Whale 11
Leopard Seal 13, 14
Minke Whale 10
mite 27
moult 13
Orca 8, 10, 11
pack ice 4, 11, 22, 24
petrels 16, 17, 22, 23
sea ice 2, 4, 11, 15, 18, 19, 24, 25
Snow Petrel 22
Southern Elephant Seal 12
Southern Giant Petrel 17
Sperm Whale 8, 9
Tardigrades 26, 27
toothed whales 8, 11, 16
Wandering Albatross 16
Water Bears 26
Weddell Seal 14
whale hunting 6, 10, 28
Wilsons Storm Petrel 23

Further reading

A. Fothergill, 1993. *Life in the Freezer: a Natural History of the Antarctic*. BBC Books, London.

Reader's Digest, 1985. *Antarctica: Great Stories from the Frozen Continent*. Reader's Digest, Sydney.

M. Norman, 2006. *The Penguin Book: Birds in Suits*. Black Dog Books, Melbourne.

Websites

www.aad.gov.au
www.antarctica.ac.uk
www.antarcticanz.govt.nz
www.greenpeace.org
www.sanap.org.za

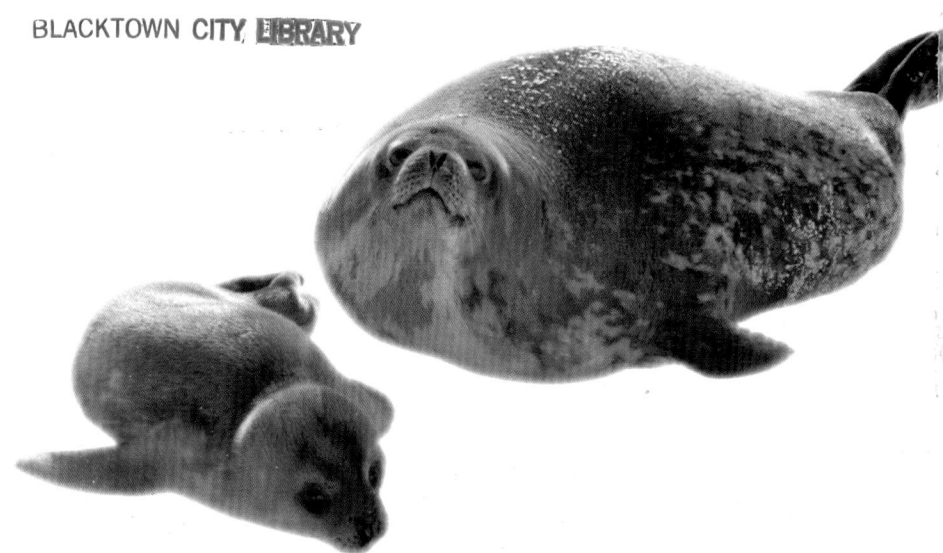

Antarctica and the future

Antarctica needs our help. We may live a long distance away, but the way we live is affecting Antarctica. Our lifestyles, the energy we use and the things we buy can all add to global warming. Global warming is reaching Antarctica and starting to melt glaciers, ice shelves and the ice sheet. Unless we act it will affect the wonderful animals that live there.

There are things we can all do to help, like saving energy, buying less, planting trees, riding or walking instead of driving, recycling, and not using air conditioners, clothes dryers or dishwashers. Contact conservation groups for more ideas of things you can do to help.